Being Kind at School

by Brienna Rossiter

FOCUS
READERS.

PIONEER

www.focusreaders.com

Focus Readers is distributed by North Star Editions: sales@northstareditions.com | 888-417-0195

Produced for Focus Readers by Red Line Editorial.

Photographs ©: iStockphoto, cover, 1, 20; Shutterstock Images, 4, 7 (people), 7 (school supplies), 9, 10, 12, 14, 16, 18

Library of Congress Cataloging-in-Publication Data
Names: Rossiter, Brienna, author.
Title: Being kind at school / by Brienna Rossiter.
Description: Lake Elmo, MN : Focus Readers, 2021. | Series: Spreading
    kindness | Includes index. | Audience: Grades 2-3
Identifiers: LCCN 2020033527 (print) | LCCN 2020033528 (ebook) | ISBN
    9781644936795 (hardcover) | ISBN 9781644937150 (paperback) | ISBN
    9781644937877 (pdf) | ISBN 9781644937518 (ebook)
Subjects: LCSH: Schools--Juvenile literature. | School
    environment--Juvenile literature. | Kindness--Juvenile literature. |
    Listening--Juvenile literature.
Classification: LCC LB1513 .R674 2021 (print) | LCC LB1513 (ebook) | DDC
    370.15/8--dc23
LC record available at https://lccn.loc.gov/2020033527
LC ebook record available at https://lccn.loc.gov/2020033528

Printed in the United States of America
Mankato, MN
012021

About the Author

Brienna Rossiter is a writer and editor who lives in Minnesota. She loves cooking food and being outside.

Table of Contents

Sight words
live out people
who work

ge
us

Chapter 1

Show Respect

People spend a lot of time together at school. It is important to treat others with **respect**. This shows you care about what they think and feel.

For example, go to the back of a line. Don't cut in front of others. Instead, wait your turn. Waiting shows respect for the people who got there first.

Take turns using books and games. Don't keep them all for yourself. Instead, choose to share. Remember that others want to use them, too.

Ways to Help Others

Sharing Space

Think about spaces you share. How could you help take good care of them? You could put books back on shelves. You could push in chairs around tables. You could help clean up. These actions keep the space nice for others.

Chapter 2

Listen Well

Pay attention when other people are talking. Don't talk at the same time. Also, listen closely to what people are saying. Don't just think about what you will say next.

Look at people while they are talking. This helps show they are important to you. And don't **interrupt** others. Instead, wait for them to finish before you **reply**.

Chapter 3

Speak Carefully

When you speak, choose kind words. Don't pick on others. Don't **gossip**. And be careful when you joke or tease. You could hurt someone's feelings.

Some people might say mean things about you. But you don't have to be mean back. You can choose to be kind instead. Your words can **encourage** others.

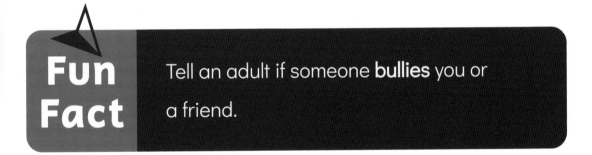

Fun Fact

Tell an adult if someone **bullies** you or a friend.

Chapter 4

Include Others

No one likes to feel left out. You can help others feel **included**. Invite people to sit with you at lunch. Or ask them to join your game.

You can help others include people, too. Speak up if your classmates are being unkind. Remind them that it's not okay. Ask them to treat others how they would like to be treated.

Fun Fact
Using kind words can help you make new friends.

FOCUS ON

Being Kind
at School

Write your answers on a separate piece of paper.

1. Write a sentence describing a kind thing you could do at school.

2. Do you find it easier to talk or listen? Why?

3. What is one way to be a good listener?
   - A. Look at the person who is talking.
   - B. Never look at the person who is talking.
   - C. Interrupt the other person.

4. What is one example of including others?
   - A. raising your hand before talking
   - B. inviting a classmate to play tag with you
   - C. reading a book by yourself

Answer key on page 24.

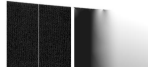

Glossary

bullies
Hurts, scares, or says mean things to others.

encourage
To give help or support.

gossip
To share unkind stories about other people.

included
Made part of a group.

interrupt
To start talking while someone else is still talking.

polite
Showing good manners.

reply
To say something back.

respect
Care for someone's thoughts and feelings.

To Learn More

BOOKS

Bassier, Emma. *Manners at School.* Minneapolis: Abdo Publishing, 2020.

Merk, T. M. *Adventure to Ava's School: Respecting Authority.* Mankato, MN: The Child's World, 2018.

NOTE TO EDUCATORS

Visit **www.focusreaders.com** to find lesson plans, activities, links, and other resources related to this title.

Index

Answer Key: **1.** Answers will vary; **2.** Answers will vary; **3.** A; **4.** B